HEALING
From
HEAVEN

HEALING
FROM
HEAVEN

Suzanne R. Jamail, Ph.D.

 ENROUTE

© En Route Books & Media, 2017
5705 Rhodes Avenue, St. Louis, MO 63109
Contact us at contactus@enroutebooksandmedia.com
Find En Route online at www.enroutebooksandmedia.com

Cover design by TJ Burdick, cover image credits:

Sky background on front page: jari, "sky" via morguefile:
http://morguefile.com/creative/jari/1/all

Sky background on back cover: Erean "Hot air Balloon"
(modified) http://morguefile.com/search/morguefile/2/sky/pop

Hardcover credits:
Angel on Front flap: blOndeeo2, "Angel" Via flikr CC:
https://flic.kr/p/5YdZxf

Angel on back cover: magnoid, "angel at the graveyard" via
flikr CC: https://flic.kr/p/5EUURx

Hardback ISBN: 978-1-63337-152-1
Paperback ISBN: 978-1-63337-153-8
E-book ISBN: 978-1-63337-154-5

Printed in the United States of America

To Jo-Ann and Charles Jamail, my parents,
whose love has given me a glimpse of heaven.

ACKNOWLEDGEMENTS

First, I would like to thank Cathy Cooke, for walking beside me in good times and bad. It is a joyous privilege to be your friend.

Carla Cheza, for your friendship and continued support, thank you.

I am forever thankful to Karen Niemela, for equal portions of kindness and encouragement.

Dr. Amie Taylor, I am thankful for your friendship.

Jim Stovall, I am profoundly grateful for your encouragement and direction.

Sebastian Mahfood, publisher and editor, for your gentle and skillful guidance, many, many thanks.

Bremen, my beautiful German Shepherd, thank you for your love, friendship, and loyal companionship.

Saint Teresa of Calcutta, who touched my life at an early age. She said: "Give yourself fully to God. He will use you to accomplish great things on the condition that you believe much more in His love than in your weakness."

I would like to express my love and appreciation to my sisters, Cindy, Jackie, and Judy. I am happy to be walking this path with you.

And most of all, my heavenly Father, thank you for hovering over me.

CONTENTS

,

FOREWORD

What a joy to read the messages allegedly from the Holy Spirit to Dr. Suzanne Jamail compiled under the title of *Healing from Heaven*!

How often we read in Scripture about how much God wants to talk to His people. We usually interpret this "speaking" to be a metaphor. However, throughout the centuries of Christian life, followers of Jesus have told of wonderful words, sometimes audible, but usually "in their hearts," consoling and inspiring them!

"Everything is received according to the nature of the recipient," wrote St. Thomas Aquinas. In the case of *Healing from Heaven*, the recipient is a strong believer in Jesus who is also a clinical psychologist. This enables Dr. Jamail to express what the Holy Spirit is telling her in a way that is sensitive to the nature of human personality.

Readers will not be shocked to read anything "off the wall" that you would think could never come from the Holy Spirit!

It happens that I myself have gotten such "messages" throughout the years. It seems as if the Holy Spirit knows the plight of high-energy professionals who are busy helping others in one way or another all the time. Everything we do is for the good, but we, ourselves, can become too frazzled to drink in the healing peace Jesus wants so much for us to experience.

Your slowly meditating on Dr. Jamail's *Healing from Heaven* could be just the start you need for the next phase in your spiritual life!

Ronda Chervin, Ph.D. is a professor of philosophy, recently retired from Holy Apostles College and Seminary, and author of numerous books about Catholic spirituality.

INTRODUCTION
THE ORIGIN OF THIS BOOK

I would briefly like to tell you how this book came into existence. It is my private journal, written during a difficult period of my life. The economy was poor, business was slow. The recession ravaged my private practice as a clinical psychologist. Thrown overboard into a sea of the unknown and the unstable, I fell into unrest and was plagued with thoughts of "going under," but in my heart, I believed my situation would turn around.

In 2013, my office building finally sold. It was located in Flint, Michigan, the crime capital of the United States. It sold for the price of a fully loaded compact car. The financial loss only served to fuel the tidal wave of disempowering thoughts that tormented me.

Giving up wasn't an option, while it frequently crossed my mind. Surely heaven understood my condition. So, I decided to say yes to life expecting God's favor to lift me above my personal challenges.

3

A reader may think all of this comes from my unconscious mind, the vault of dreams, intuitions, and buried beliefs. I don't think so. I believe my book came from our Creator because I asked God to give me a new assignment. At that point, I believe I formed a creative alliance with the Holy Spirit, who spoke directly to my heart.

A SUGGESTION TO THE READER

Take your time as you read these spiritual passages. This book is not meant to be read in a single session or even within a few days. These spiritual passages do not need to be read in the order in which they are presented. The table of contents gives you an idea which passage might be most beneficial to you.

May this book be instrumental in helping you find joy and fulfillment in the face of life's challenges.

Suzanne R. Jamail, Ph.D.

5

Deposition of Christ by Paolo Veronese (1548-9)

ABANDON INTO GOD'S EMBRACE

God will take care of you. He loves you and draws you near with an embrace of welcome. Reach for Him. Jesus lived to do the will of His father. We, too, are called to say yes to God. Accept whatever He gives and accept whatever He takes. Anchor yourself in His loving embrace. Let Him do a work in you.

God provides. His tender love envelops you. God is in control. Whatever comes into your life, quit resisting, quit fighting. God will use every circumstance to your advantage when you stay in an attitude of faith.

The Destruction of Leviathan, Gustave Doré (1866)

ANXIETY

You pray in a moment bordering on panic. The Lord speaks to you and assures you that He will give you grace to handle tomorrow when it comes. These words are not your own. You worry endlessly about tomorrow, the present moment eluding you. The incessant mental noise torments you. Your internal dialogue is negative and harmful. You long for mental quietude.

Believe God is in control over your life. Learn to relax and accept where you are: Don't resist no matter what comes your way. Trust God and rest in His grace. Cast your cares.

Your situation is formidable, but heaven knows your needs. Open the door to your heart, where your loving Father dwells. Trust in Him. Rest in Him, cast your cares, and decide to live in peace. Choose to embrace each day for every day is special. There is no such thing as an ordinary day. God will give you what you need one day at a time. Cast your cares.

Newton by William Blake (1795)

BE YOURSELF

Focus on your unique strengths. God wants you to feel good about yourself just as you are. You are unique. You were made as you are on purpose. You have everything you need to fulfill your purpose. God doesn't make mistakes. The final chapter of your life hasn't been written. Keep a good attitude. Be patient. God is molding you.

In general, you have been a busy person. You are excessively disciplined, perfectionistic, and conscientious. You fear being found inadequate. The unknown is terrifying. Why is this happening? Others are unaware of your plight, for they see you as a super man or woman. But you are ordinary. You are ordinary. The false self, the persona you fabricated to be affirmed and accepted by significant others is being peeled away. You fear intimidation, rejection, and punishment; your outside world can't help you.

Mastering your demons through your intellect isn't possible. It is time to face your true nature. You have something to offer the world no one else can. Your identity is ego-oriented and the dismantling of your life only serves to exacerbate your teetering self-regard. You are thirsty for God, desperate in search of your own true uniqueness. You are on the potter's wheel. God is the potter and you are the clay. Through your trials, He is refining you.

Three Graces by Raphael Sanzio (1501-1505)

CONTENTMENT

With the storms and stress of life, it's easy to forget what is going right and dwell on that which isn't. Choose to have a positive frame of mind. Trust God and keep a good attitude. Contentment starts in your attitude.

You are determined to be positive, hopeful, and trusting, believing God is watching over you. You are learning to accept your situation, resisting serves no useful purpose. You are where you are for a reason. Your challenge is to embrace this place believing God has something better for you, if you stay faithful and keep pressing forward.

Slowly, begin to see yourself coming up higher, rising to a new level. Picture yourself happy, positive, and relaxed, living an abundant life. When negative, discouraging thoughts surface, turn to God. Keep your mind set on God and thoughts that give birth to growth.

Beatrice Addressing Dante by William Blake (1824-1827)

FAITH

Life is a constant cycle of change; ups and downs are a given. God calls you to persevere no matter what trials and adversities come your way. You have seeds of greatness in you. There is nothing that will cross your path that you and God together can't handle.

You are connected to a divine source, created in God's image. Stay in faith, honoring God, trusting Him. God is in every detail of your life. Nothing that you are facing is a surprise to Him. Don't give up. Shake off discouragement, disappointment, and defeat. Persevere and keep a good attitude. Move in faith and know God is by your side.

Sometimes, despite your best efforts, life seems to unravel. Sometimes doors close, because doors of opportunity are opening around the corner. Look at setbacks as temporary. Look at them as opportunities to grow and heal. Nothing comes our way without a purpose. When you get knocked down by life, get up and stay aligned with God. With God on your side you are always greater than your obstacles.

The Parable of the Wise and Foolish Virgins
by William Blake (c. 1825)

SURRENDER

When trials and difficulties come, learn to get in agreement with God. He is refining you, changing you, ridding you of impurities. There is a divine purpose for every challenge you face. Adversities strengthen character and test faith. Trust God and keep a good attitude, staying faithful where you are.

When you decide to develop an intimacy with God, you know you are transformed. You are looking for a complete overhaul: a mind at peace, and a joyful spirit. God is within you, holding you, protecting you. He is nudging you to relax and simply be. He is never imposing. His ways are gentle. You must be humble enough to realize it isn't possible to be in charge of all things all the time.

Let go of your agenda and let God lead. Trust Him and pray. Prayer allows you to stay in the present with God who speaks to you in the present. Surrender your distress and offer your inner turmoil. God's love is unconditional. As you surrender, doors of opportunity will open.

Managing your life from an intellectual perspective will keep you feeling unbalanced, busy, and anxious. Your mind tells you, you have reached your potential. Your mind will generate thoughts that are not true. Real healing, joy, and peacefulness can only occur when you go beneath the surface and enter into an interior silence with God.

St. John Restoring Dante's Sight by Gustave Doré (1868)

GIVING

You are carrier of God's love. Bring your love, kindness, and compassion to others. Be a blessing. Look for opportunities to brighten someone's day. Don't sit with your wounds. It's not about you.

There is an epidemic of self-centeredness. Relationships are exploitative, shallow, and neglectful. The excessive preoccupation with self is not how you were created. Rather, your sacred self is guided by love and authentic connections to others.

You were created to be a giver. Whatever you give will always come back to you. Especially during moments of pain and powerlessness, look for others who are hurting. Whatever you give will always come back.

The Glorification of Saint Felix and Saint Adauctus
by Carlo Innocenzo Carlone (c. 1759)

GRATITUDE

It's easy to have a grateful attitude when life is going smoothly. Challenges, obstacles, and setbacks often trigger a myriad of negative thoughts and emotional symptoms. You feel you are doing something wrong.

You were never promised a smooth journey. But trust God will journey with you. Accept what is. The difficult times will pass. Be cheerful in spirit for God is with you in chaos and calm. Adapt to life with an attitude of gratitude. Dwell on all that is good in your life. Live in appreciation. Heaven knows your needs.

Jacob's Dream by Gustave Doré (1865)

PRAYER

Dwell in the gentle healing presence of God. Spend time each day in silent communion with your heavenly Father. Be silent. Be still and know you are with God. Prayer opens your heart to God in love, friendship, and surrender.

Prayer requires daily practice. Your life changes when habits change. If you want to live a balanced, peaceful life, prayer will help you achieve this.

Go beneath the surface. Still your mind, open your heart, and pray. Pray for your loved ones and pray for strangers. Listen to God. Ask Him for guidance and turn to Him for healing. God will supply your needs. In prayer, thank God for your life, for in abundance or poverty, you are in the palm of His hand.

Our Father, who art in heaven
Hallowed be thy name
Thy kingdom come
Thy will be done, on earth as

It is in heaven.
Give us this day our daily bread.
And forgive us our trespasses, as
We forgive those who trespass
against us.
And lead us not into temptation,
But to deliver us from evil. Amen.

Descent of the Holy Spirit by Gustave Doré (1885)

SILENCE

Daily life is often noisy and busy. It's easy to feel stressed and out of balance. Learn to get quiet so God can refresh and restore you. Get alone with God and let Him cleanse your mind.

You frequently start each day feeling hurried, rushed, and under pressure. You have developed a harmful habit of rushing and have planned your days around this self-destructive pattern.

In your frantic, hurried, and noisy mind, there is little, if any, space to hear God's voice. How are you to be healthy in mind and body without a quiet centering in God? It is only when you get still and into God's presence that you will find Him.

When you rest the mind and body, ready to receive God, you move from your ego, mind-oriented preoccupations to a spiritual centering where you learn that you are precious to God and He wants to transform you if you invite Him.

The Seven Deadly Sins and the Last Four Things
by Hieronymous Bosch (c. 1500)

THOUGHTS

Your mind torments you. Negative, fearful, disempowering thoughts thrash about like a boat on choppy waters. Repetitive, dark, mental noise pulls you to the past or future. Still your mind. Control your thought life. Withdraw from you senses. Self-pity and wounds drain your life energy. Your life is determined by your thoughts.

God is not in the past, nor future. He speaks to you in the present. Accept your life, as is. Think positive, God-like thoughts. Trust you are where you are supposed to be. Say yes to life. Heaven knows your needs. Rainy days and sunny days, believe God is directing your steps.

Matelda Gathering Flowers by Gustave Doré (1868)

SIMPLICITY

Many of the props have been removed from your life. Of course, this was not of your choosing, but with fewer distractions, you realize you have the essentials to be happy, whole, and to fulfill your life's purpose. You have many small things that make your life wonderful. Your life is being reordered, pruning away the trivial, leaving room for spiritual growth. Placing less importance on contemporary living and self-centered values, you live closer to God. Be more concerned with your message than your money.

The Gates of Hell by Gustave Doré (1868)

THE UNKNOWN

You are frightened of the unknown. Anxious of what lies beyond tomorrow. You strive to bring order to this dis-order but there is no authority to guide you. Your steps are slowed and awkward. There is no rushing.

It is as if your life has been pulled into sequences. You can see yourself and all of your insecurities clearly. You hear the inner dialogue you have been running from. You demand to know the outcome. You deserve to know.

In between the anxious and despairing thoughts are flashes of joy and calm. It is you and God. He is your authority, your travel companion. Journey together and travel light for all you have is this moment.

Jesus Blessing the Children by Gustave Doré (1866)

BE LIKE CHILDREN

Children, when very young, do not think of tomorrow or yesterday. They are not burdened with thoughts of time. They play, laugh, and accept things in simplicity. They live free and light, appreciating the little things in life. They believe their parents and depend on them. God is your heavenly Father. Trust and depend on Him and you will find your peace. God is in complete control of your life.

Understand, God has a master plan for you. He uses problems to encourage you to depend on Him, trusting Him completely; there is much for you to learn. Hold onto God's hand and He will make His home in your heart.

The Wedding at Cana (detail) by Paolo Veronese (1563)

CHOOSE TO ENJOY LIFE

The future promises happiness. You tell yourself once these adverse circumstances fade, you will be happy, and joyful.

Choose to enjoy your life now. God has a customized plan for your life. It will play out in His timing, not yours. A good attitude makes the journey endurable. God's will for you is to experience joy. Your life is now, this moment. Accept it as is, trusting God who is faithful. Enjoy your life now.

The Host of Heaven by Gustave Doré (1868)

YOU ARE LOVED

You are precious to God. You are special to Him exactly as you are. He is your caring Father, loving you unconditionally. It is not what you do, or how many successes or failures you have had that matter. God knows your inherent value and wants you to be the person whom he designed you to be.

Stop focusing on mistakes and setbacks. You are worthy of your own love and self-acceptance. God loves you as evidenced by his love for his only Son.

Dante's Dream at the Time of the Death of Beatrice
by Dante Gabriel Rossetti (1871)

Accepting What Is

You resist that which is causing you distress. Sitting with your wounds, you feel powerless and defeated. It is not your circumstances though, but your attitude about these circumstances that give rise to your feelings. You decide whether or not to be happy. It is always your choice.

Your challenge is to have a cheerful heart, embracing what is. Allow this present moment to be. Appreciate and accept the ever-changing nature of life. God will order things for you. Go with the flow of life.

Oberon, Titania and Puck with Fairies Dancing
by William Blake (c. 1786)

LAUGHTER

Life is a journey spotted with satisfaction and struggle.

Enjoy where you are, looking for opportunities to laugh along the way. Laughter lightens a situation and the benefits are far-ranging.

Laughter is good medicine for mind and body. Take yourself and life less seriously. Whether you laugh alone or with others, do it often.

Life is better when you're laughing.

Virgil's Circle of Friends by Gustave Doré (1868)

THE IMPORTANCE
OF FRIENDSHIPS

Good friendships uplift and sustain you. Intimate connections are central to your existence.

Spend time with people who encourage you to reach new levels. Align yourself with positive, joy-filled people.

A good friend makes you laugh, keeps your secrets, shares your burdens and blessings, boosts your wavering self-worth, and helps you cope with hardships and challenges in life.

No matter what you are facing, it is always easier with a good friend by your side. Pour your love into your friends.

God's love is magnified when you share it. God is always with you, always your friend ... and the friend of your friend.

The Souls of our Saintly Ancestors Console Us
by Gustave Dore (1868)

DON'T GIVE UP

No matter how difficult the situation, stay in faith. Nothing is impossible with God.

Quitting is easy, but God encourages you to keep on, shaking off discouragement and defeat. Lean on Him, trusting Him to direct your steps.

Choose faith that things will change in your favor. Control your thoughts. Setbacks or bad days are inevitable. Dust yourself off and begin again.

Choose positive, God-like thoughts. Don't give up, dig deep. Correct your thinking and prune away destructive thoughts.

Your best days are not behind you. Today can be a turning point in your life.

Dante Drinking from the Eunoe by Gustave Doré (1868)

THINK POSITIVELY
ABOUT YOUR LIFE

You can master your thoughts or be a slave to them. Your life will always follow your thoughts.

Choose to focus on your blessings instead of your problems. God has a plan for your life even if you don't know what it is.

Stay in an attitude of faith expecting your situation to improve. Adverse circumstances are a part of life. A bad attitude is your choice.

Don't let your thoughts steal your joy and poison your days. Trust in God and think positively about your life.

Rescue from the Dark Wood of Error
by William Blake c. 1826

NUMBER YOUR DAYS

Don't waste your days feeling negative and discouraged. Life is far too precious and fleeting for this victim consciousness.

Make your days memorable. Each day is full of possibilities.

Use your time well: loving, living, and learning.

Choose to dwell on the many wonders in your life, realizing it's a precious privilege to be alive.

Relax and accept where you are. God is in control over your life, always. Tomorrow is never promised to you.

So be mindful about how you're spending your days. Each day God invites you to be a better version of yourself.

Smile, laugh, and ride the waves of life. Your lifeguard walks on water.

Dante and Virgil Climbing Heavenward
by Gustave Doré (1868)

TRAVERSING LIFE'S MOUNTAINS

Life is a journey. Give it your best, trusting God to journey with you. No challenge has any power over you because you believe God is in complete control. He wants you to be positive.

Keep a good attitude, smile, and live with energy and passion. You have a lot to be thankful for.

Focus on your blessings and cast your cares. No matter your circumstances, believe all things are possible with God. Trials, tribulations, and disappointments are necessary. Without challenges there is no need for faith.

Go with the flow of life. God orders things for you.

Live in appreciation, saying yes to life. Learn to enjoy the journey on your way to the summit.

The Deluge by Michaelangelo di
Lodovico Buonarroti Simoni (1510)

WHY

It's all so frustrating and confusing at times. Your plans haven't worked out. Why did this happen to you?

Trust God wants you here, now. Accept your life as is, even though you have unanswered questions. God will direct your path if you relax and let Him lead.

Stop asking why. Many of your questions will remain unanswered.

Learn to accept that you don't have all the answers. Trust that God's plan for your life is much better than yours.

Live passionately and purposely. God has figured out all the details.

Stop asking why. Trust.

The Book of Job by William Blake (1821)

It Isn't Fair

You worked hard, obeying God and everything fell apart anyway. You feel sorry for yourself because it isn't fair.

Press on, believing God will turn your situation around. It isn't fair, but God is. It's a time of reconsideration.

Stay in faith, learn to trust Him in a greater way, and be patient. God still has a plan for your life and will use your trials to promote you. There is a purpose for every problem.

Believe you are being prepared for greater things. Every trial is used to develop your character.

Do your part and God will open the right doors for you. Your problems will make you better or bitter. The choice is yours.

Dante gazes fixedly at Beatrice and every other thought is banished from his mind by Gustave Doré (1868)

LOVE

You are created to live a life of love. Love the Lord your God with all your heart and soul, love yourself, and others.

Your relationships are what matter most to God. It's not your career, your material possessions, or money that are of importance. You were created to love and be loved.

You bring glory to God when you live your life with love. Life is so much brighter and fuller when you're motivated by love. To nurture your relationships is to live joyfully. And to do so will bring many blessings.

Give your love abundantly.

The Blessed Souls Forming an Eagle in the Sky
Gustav Doré (1868)

BE A BLESSING

You were created to make a contribution with your life. You have a specific assignment that only you can fulfill. You are an original, a custom-made masterpiece, fully equipped to fulfill His purposes. Just like all of God's creations.

Regardless of your career, your true calling is that of service. You are here to be a blessing to others. Small acts of kindness are as important as large ones.

Look for ways to serve and give. Trust God and keep serving faithfully. Your gifts and talents have been given to you to glorify God.

Whatever you give, do so with love. You have been sent to serve.

Arachne by Gustave Doré (1868)

THINK OF YOURSELF LESS

You are called to think about others as well as yourself. You are here to glorify God. Be cheerfully devoted to God and let Him use you to help the troubled, lonely, and lost.

When it comes to healing you are always faced with two choices: ego or soul.

Your ego, or self-esteem is in constant search of praise and bolstering, and is in endless pursuit of recognition. It hungers for any morsel of external or worldly acknowledgement. But there is no satisfying the ego, because its hunger is insatiable. It needs to be fed in order to survive.

On the other hand, the soul seeks to serve and the less self-focus, the more you can hear God's whispers in the trees, flowers, and streams, assuring you that all will be fine.

Choose to live selflessly and generously, seeking the face of God in everyone and everything.

The Creation of Adam
by Michaelangelo di Lodovico Buonarroti Simoni (1510)

ARE YOU THERE, GOD?

At times, you feel abandoned by God. He seems to have slipped away and you wonder what has caused the estrangement. God never leaves you but sometimes you can't feel Him because your relationship is deepening. It feels like He went away.

The crisis of faith opens you to alternatives, which may strengthen you. Will you continue to follow Him when He doesn't feel near? God is always just a breath away, even when you can't feel His presence.

Will you continue your friendship with God, loving Him, trusting Him, and serving Him during this period of perceived abandonment?

Your relationship with God is being nourished at a deeper level. He is with you. He is in control. You are held. God is ever faithful.

The First Day of Creation
by Michaelangelo di Lodovico Buonarroti Simoni (1510)

LIFE IS A JOURNEY AND GOD HOLDS THE MAP

You strive for order, structure, predictability and think you possess control over your life. This is the ego's illusion.

In truth, you are powerless over your life as God designed you for His purposes. He will open doors, close doors, allowing rain and sunshine throughout your days. He asks that you allow Him to do a work in you and follow Him. His ways are never imposing; He will never force you to do something against your will.

While you may not understand the path you find yourself on, trust you are exactly where you are supposed to be. Every obstacle, every mountain, every challenge is for a higher purpose.

Nothing comes your way without God's permission. He knows your destination and His path holds many wonders.

Matilda Immerses Dante in Lethe by Gustave Doré (1868)

LET GO OF THE PAST

Yesterday is gone. Today is a new day, full of wonder, begin again.

Don't let the past dampen your passion for today. Let go of the past so you can receive today with enthusiasm. If you want to experience God's abundant blessings, your mind must release its focus on pain from the past. Your life will always follow your thoughts. If you focus on pain, that is what you perpetuate. You will never experience happiness with a mind compulsively retracing the past.

Let go of the past and expect God to restore and renew you. Your best days are in front of you.

Angel of the Church before the Door of Purgatory
by Gustave Doré (1868)

FORGIVENESS

Decide to let go of bitterness, anger, and resentment.

Forgive yourself and those who have wronged you. You can't experience God's best with a heart full of grievance.

Decide to embrace forgiveness and open yourself to receive God's blessings. You were made to be tenderhearted and kind, not unmerciful and uncaring.

Decide to embrace forgiveness.

Heavenly host singing Gloria in Excelsis
by Gustave Doré (1868)

ARE YOU CELEBRATING OR COMPLAINING?

Life is to be celebrated, not tolerated. What are you choosing?

Be mindful of your thoughts for they give rise to peacefulness or pain. You will never experience happiness with an undisciplined mind.

If left unmanaged, your mind will generate chaos and confusion, casting a dark indiscernible path.

Guard your thoughts for they are shaping your life.

The Host of Myriad Glowing Souls
by Gustave Doré (1868)

LIVING HIS PURPOSE

God has a purpose for your life even He hasn't told you. You have a unique destiny to fulfill. You are called to be what He created you to be. This may be markedly different from what the world expects you to be.

Walk with Him, serving others, and radiating God's love.

Embrace your purpose with arms wide open.

Live your life as a prayer and give God the glory.

Band of Souls around the Wall of Rock
by Gustave Doré (1868)

PATIENCE

You are called to cheerfully persevere during trying conditions. Life is about accepting what unfolds and walking the path of God.

Suppress your urge to complain and express resentment and dissatisfaction.

Practice patience, accepting with calmness, challenges, delays, and troubles.

Believe that God has a purpose for your problems. Trust Him and His timing. Your problems have a purpose and God is always at work in your life. God is in control.

The Souls of the Just Circling to Form Letters
by Gustave Doré (1868)

SAVOR YOUR STEPS

Slow down, breathe, and surrender to the flow of life.

Resist the urge to rush through your days. See how much brighter and fuller life becomes.

Say yes to life, living with appreciation for every day is special.

Boldly step into this day, savoring your steps, walking in faith.

The Last Judgment (detail of the Redeemed)
by Michaelangelo di Lodovico Buonarroti Simoni (1510)

JOY

Choose to enjoy your life. Delight in being alive. There are many tiny miracles every day.

Thank God for your blessings. Find reasons to smile, laugh, and love, embracing life.

A God-centered life is a deepening collaborative relationship. God delights when you grow in His grace and lovingly fills you with joy.

Surrender your brokenness and let His light and love transform you.

The sparkling circles of the heavenly host
by Gustave Doré (1868)

PEACE

God wants you to feel at peace in your heart no matter the external circumstances. Life is unpredictable and the unknown is daunting.

Stay close to God, knowing you are in His hands, His love and protection are unfailing. Let God be your center and He will give you peace during any storm. He will build your faithfulness.

Step closer to Him where you will find your peace.

Release your desire to control and order your life. Understand, you are in the palm of His hand.

Cast your cares, rest, and find your peace.

The Dream of Saint Helena by Paolo Veronese (c. 1570)

DARE TO DREAM

You are not who you were when this journey began. Serial setbacks and storms left you broken and suffering. Life struck you down and there was nothing more you could do in your own strength to alter the course. So, in a moment of desperation, you hotheadedly prayed and God surprisingly answered.

Instantly, you knew God had been waiting for you, welcoming you into His loving embrace. God was in control. He has always been in control, involved in every detail of your life. Nothing you experienced was a surprise to Him. He's the creator of the universe! He used every trial, every struggle, and every setback to refine you, change you, and transform you.

God was cementing your faith but you continued to stand firm in your conviction that you could manage your life on your own terms. There were gentle pushes to relax and simply be, but you kept struggling, stumbling, proudly rejecting divine assistance.

Worn out beyond repair, you surrendered to God offering

your inner turmoil. Stilling your mind and opening your heart, you prayed, asking God to supply your needs and to heal you. You have moved from your ego and mind- oriented preoccupations to a God-centered collaborative friendship.

Your best days are now. This is your time of tremendous harvest.

The Saintly Throng in the Shape of a Rose
by Gustave Doré (1868)

DECLARE YOUR DREAMS

Stay passionate about seeing your dreams materialize. God restores splintered dreams, but you must stay in faith, trusting Him, and choosing to enjoy your life now. Embrace each day with enthusiasm.

Live in appreciation that no day is ordinary. Look for ways to be a blessing to others. Whatever you give, do so with love. God rewards excellence.

Dreams from God are unstoppable. Declare your dreams. Dream big, for nothing is impossible with God. Live with confidence, believing you will triumph in God's timing. You are sailing the sea of life. God is at the helm of your ship, steering your voyage. He is responsible for the safe navigation during stormy seas, inclement weather, and in times of quietude and calm.

CPSIA information can be obtained
at www.ICGtesting.com
Printed in the USA
BVOW07*2020090117
473028BV00001B/1/P

9 781633 371521